Living Your Legacy
Design a Life of Purpose and Impact

Table of Contents

The purpose of life is not to be happy. It is to be useful, to be honorable, to be compassionate, to have it make some difference that you have lived and lived well.

— Ralph Waldo Emerson

Chapter 1. Introduction

Welcome to the exploratory journey of your lifetime, defined by intense meaning and profound impact—welcome to 'Living Your Legacy: Design a Life of Purpose and Impact'. This Special Report unearths the luminous potential residing inside you and stirringly champions your transformation into an individual whose life reverberates with purpose, whose actions inspire and whose legacy reflects the grand narrative of a truly lived life. Becoming the architect of your fate, embodying values that define you, and making choices that will etch your name in the sands of time—this isn't confined to the pages of heroic tales, but can be your reality. We wholly believe that the brightest version of you is yet to become, and this report is the torchbearer of that journey. Embark on this transformative voyage with us, and awaken the part of you that aches to make a difference. Reading this inspiring special report might just be your first step towards living the legacy you were meant to leave behind!

Chapter 2. Setting the Foundation: Identifying Your Core Values

Before we initiate this monumental journey towards crafting a life of lasting significance, we must establish a strong, resilient foundation from which to build. Our core values are the fundamental beliefs that serve as the basis of our identity, shaping our perception, guiding our actions, shaping our reactions, and inspiring our passions. They permeate every facet of our lives, exuding subtle influence over the decisions that sculpt our destiny. A seed planted in the fertile soil of self-discovery, these values sprout into the defining factors that add purpose to our existence and bring into focus the legacy we wish to craft. These intrinsic principles continuously evolve with us, refining our character and moulding our life's path in the process.

2.1. Unraveling the Essence of Core Values

The task of identifying our core values might seem daunting at first. Fear not, as it's a process of coming home to oneself. When we strip away the external influences of societal pressures, familial expectations, and cultural norms, what lies at the heart of our being are our core values. They can be seen as the compass by which we navigate the turbulent seas of life. This inner compass guides us steadfastly towards our true North, keeping us on course towards the vision we aspire to manifest. It outlines the principles we refuse to compromise on, the passions we willingly risk everything for, and the virtues we choose to uphold above all else.

2.2. The Process of Identifying Core Values

Identifying your core values is akin to excavating precious gems. It requires patience, introspective insight, and a willingness to confront and embrace all the facets that make you, uniquely you. Embark on this journey, keeping in mind that your aim is not to create an impressive list, but to distill the essence of who you are and who you aim to become.

Consider the moments when you felt authentically 'you', vibrant with purpose and contentment. What values were you upholding during these instances? Contrarily, identify the times you felt discomfort or regret. What values were being ignored or violated then? On this introspective quest, you might discover values rooted in love, truth, integrity, courage, freedom, or compassion, among others. The key is to remain honest and open, unearthing the deep-seated values that resonate profoundly with your core.

2.3. The Importance of Core Values in Living Your Legacy

Understanding our core values is pivotal in determining the legacy we wish to leave. They form the bedrock of our actions, decisions, and commitments, often illustrating what we deem most important in our lives. Living in alignment with our core values brings profound fulfilness, igniting a sense of inner harmony and adding discernible purpose to our existence. It not only ensures that our actions and decisions are congruent with our true selves but also serves as a guiding light in turbulent times, aiding in decision-making and conflict resolution.

Conversely, living a life that is misaligned with our core values could lead to disconnection, unhappiness, and regret. It's akin to building a skyscraper on a shaky foundation—it's bound to crumble.

Their pivotal role in constructing our lives makes core values the premise upon which we 'live' our legacy every day. They serve as markers guiding our journey, ensuring that our daily actions reflect the kind of person we strive to be and the impact we aspire to have on the world around us.

Our core values should not merely exist in our private thoughts. They should permeate our actions, suffuse our relationships, imbue our work and seep into every part of our being. It's only then that we truly initiate the journey of 'Living Your Legacy'.

This chapter encapsulates the amino acids of personal evolution; the core values. The subsequent chapters offer a detailed guide on mastering the art of bringing your values to life, crafting a vision that aligns with your deepest truths, infusing evolution and growth in your journey, and becoming the glowing beacon of transformation that signals purpose and impact in your wake. They will set your foot firmly on the path of living a life that's full, radiant with authenticity, sparkling with integrity and inspiring in its legacy. Today, you step upon this path, not merely as a traveler, but as a conscious and purposeful creator of your legacy.

Chapter 3. Creating Your Vision: The Blueprint of Your Legacy

Creating a vision is the essence of building a legacy. It is a roadmap that provides direction, a plan that informs action, and a dream that inspires effort. Only by having a clear vision can you design and craft a legacy that reflects who you truly aspire to be. You need to envision the kind of person you want to become, the values you want to uphold, and the impact you hope to have on the world. With that vision, you will be empowered to make it reality, modeling your actions today to reflect the legacy you want to create tomorrow.

3.1. Envisioning Your Ideal Self

Reflect on the person you want to be. It's about outlining the qualities you wish to embody, the values you want to uphold, and the actions you envision taking. Your ideal self is an aspiration, a paradigm of perfection. This is not about striving to be better than others, but about being the best version of yourself. Keep it realistic, but don't limit your aspirations. Your ideal self should challenge you, pushing you towards continuous growth and self-improvement.

Here's the method to go about creating your vision:

1. Write down your top ten ideal qualities.

2. For each quality, write three actions that embody it.

3. Prioritize your list according to what resonates most with you.

Remember, these are not tasks to complete, but behaviors to emulate. They form the essence of your vision and your eventual legacy.

3.2. Building the Blueprint of Your Legacy

Just as an architect creates a blueprint before starting a construction project, so should you design a plan for your legacy. You've identified your ideal qualities and behaviors, now put them into a broader context. Your legacy blueprint should outline your grand goals, the impact you desire to have, and the people you aim to inspire.

1. Identify your major goals: what do you want to achieve?
2. Map out the broader impact of these goals: who will be affected and how?
3. Identify how your ideal qualities and actions will aid in achieving these goals.

Your blueprint should inspire you, serving as a living document that can evolve with you as you grow.

3.3. Moving From Vision to Action

Converting a vision from an abstract thought into reality is the most challenging part. It's the bridge that connects who you are to who you wish to become, leading you from present realities to future possibilities.

At this stage, break down your overall vision into bite-sized, actionable steps. Focus on developing actionable plans for each quality and goal you've mapped in your blueprint. Use SMART goals (Specific, Measurable, Achievable, Relevant, and Time-bound) to set your action plans.

Remember, the journey of a legacy is a marathon, not a sprint. Patience and persistence are key in moving from vision to action. Success is not measured by the speed but by the direction.

3.4. Adjusting Your Sails: Embracing Change

Life is never linear, and neither will your journey towards your legacy be. Change is the only constant. To navigate it effectively, you need to be flexible and adapt, adjusting your sails as the winds of life shift. Be open to revising your blueprint and adaptable to opportunities of growth or unforeseen circumstances.

While your vision might be stable, the path leading to it might necessitate alterations. Remember that these changes are not an indication of failure, but markers of growth and maturity. Your blueprint should be flexible, allowing for adjustments while still fostering progress in the general direction of your vision.

Creating your vision for your legacy might seem daunting initially, but it is a journey that will define the kind of person you will become. It is about finding your purpose, embracing your potential, and making a positive impact. It is about moving beyond existence, making choices that resonate with who you are, and ultimately, becoming an inspiration for others. By creating your vision and following your blueprint, you pave the road to living the legacy you were meant to leave behind.

Your journey starts here. Your legacy awaits.

Chapter 4. Unleashing the Hero Within: The Power of Personal Evolution

Every single one of us, illuminated under the ethereal glow of existence, carries within a hidden hero—an entity of extraordinary potential and profound wisdom—merely aching to be released. It exists at the foundation of our beings, punctuating our stories with moments of courage, resilience, and self-belief. However, perennially latent, it requires a gentle nudge, a slight awakening to become an active participant in our life's trajectory. This chapter delves into the realms of personal evolution and charts a comprehensive journey that empowers us to realize, nurture, and release the dormant hero that lies within.

4.1. The Hero's Conception: Discovering Our Potential

The genesis of a hero begins with the delicate acknowledgment of our unique potential. We have been endowed with a variegated palette of talents, abilities, and strengths, often tucked away in inconspicuous corners of our consciousness. A tedious process, unravelling these aspects involves introspective exploration chaperoned by humility and curiosity. Think of it as archaeology of the self, where we carefully extricate the fragments of our potential, polish them with acceptance, and piece them together to form a discernible profile of who we are and who we could be.

4.2. The Hero's Initiation: Embracing Self-belief

Believing in oneself is the first step towards the heroic tale of personal evolution. Self-belief is the invisible force propelling us towards unimaginable summits. It fuels our will to pursue our purpose, guides us through tough terrains, and bolsters our determination in the face of setbacks. To let our inner hero emerge and thrive, we need to nurture our self-belief, watering it with positive affirmation, cultivating it through small victories, and safeguarding it from the frost of self-doubt.

4.3. The Hero's Journey: Navigating through Change

As with every epic journey, the hero's quest is suffused with trials and challenges. Behavioral changes, breaking free from limiting beliefs, and forging new, resilient paths are central to this journey of evolution. The process might seem daunting at first, but when we choose courage over comfort, growth over stagnation, we inch closer to our heroic identity. Equipped with flexibility, patience, and the power of self-reflection, we journey through transformation, understanding that personal evolution is a continuous, life-long journey and not a finite destination.

4.4. Hero's Armor: Building Resilience

Crafting resilience is an integral part of our metamorphosis into our heroic selves. An armor that shields us from adversities, resilience empowers us to bounce back from setbacks with increased vigor and a refined perspective. It enables us to navigate through life's uncertainties with confidence and optimism, transforming adversities into stepping stones towards victory. Strengthening resilience requires consistent efforts, like cultivating a growth mindset, learning from failures, and developing emotional intelligence.

4.5. Empowering the Hero: Nurturing Growth Mindset

A growth mindset is the hero's most powerful weapon. It inspires us to perceive challenges as opportunities for growth, to embrace failures as learning platforms, and to perceive effort as the pathway to mastery. This mindset is the catalyst for personal evolution, enabling us to morph our awareness, actions, and attitudes in a direction that ultimately serves our growth and actualizes our potential. Cultivating a growth mindset involves rewiring existing thought patterns, embracing a love for learning, and replacing the fear of failure with the courage to try.

4.6. The Hero's Triumph: Mastery through Consistent Effort

The hero within is the culmination of our deliberate, sustained efforts towards self-improvement. Embracing our imperfections, extracting wisdom from failures, and channeling our strengths towards consistent growth helps us inch closer to actualizing our evolving selves. The key lies in relentless pursuit, acknowledging that mastery is not about perfection, but persistent progress. We awaken our inner hero when we cease to shy away from our vulnerabilities and instead see them as facets to explore, understand, and transform.

Unleashing the hero within is an empowering journey that celebrates personal evolution. As we embark on the journey of self-discovery, nurturing self-belief, resilience, and a growth mindset, we create a life that is rich in purpose, abundant in growth, and reflective of our highest potential. The beauty of this journey is that it paints our everyday life with hues of the extraordinary, transforming our existing narrative into an impactful saga that is continuously being written, enriched, and celebrated.

Chapter 5. Consistent Growth: Mastering the Art of Perseverance

Among the critical elements propelling us towards a life endowed with purpose and change-making impact, the role of consistent growth is paramount, akin to a silent powerhouse. Through the embodiment of perpetual growth—fueled by perseverance—we morph into relentless, prosperous, and formidable influencers of change. Such consistent growth is the key to unlocking an undeniable legacy—one that echoes through time and space.

5.1. The Intricate Nature of Consistent Growth

To understand the true essence of consistent growth, one needs to appreciate its multifaceted nature. It is not a single event, nor a magical turnaround happening overnight. Indeed, it is an intricate blend of numerous interwoven threads. Whether it is honing an existing skill or learning something completely new, every step you take towards development contributes to this growth metric.

In a society that celebrates instant gratification, learning to appreciate small advancements over significant periods can indeed be challenging. Yet, true growth involves embracing such minuscule yet momentous progress. You must relish each step, every mistake, and all the tiny victories. Through this continuous cycle of learning, unlearning, and relearning, you breed constancy in your growth trajectory, which ultimately culminates in your legacy.

5.2. Firm Roots in Perseverance

However, this constant commitment towards growth is not an easy path to tread. It demands persistence and patience—the twin pillars propelling one's growth journey. Without patient persistence, the heartening allure of consistent growth can quickly fade away as life inevitably throws hurdles your way.

Here, the role of perseverance blooms. It does not imply a lack of obstacles or hindrances but rather signifies the capacity to persist through them, to rise every time you fall, and to harbor the gusto to move forward despite torrential odds. Conditioning oneself to perceive challenges as stepping stones rather than obstacles instills the mindset that invigorates perseverance.

5.3. Impact of Individual Growth on Collective Progress

Perseverance-driven growth doesn't only impact the individual. It lavishly trickles down, contributing to the progress of those around you and the community at large. By showcasing the tenacity to persist and grow, you set a motivating precedent, encouraging others towards the path of constant self-evolution. It empowers those in your circle of influence to seek out their development and growth, thus spawning a cascading effect that echoes through the community.

Take a moment to reflect on the butterfly effect—a tiny disturbance creating significant impact. Such is the potential of your growth, emboldened by perseverance. It prompts a ripple effect, fostering a growth mindset, and birthing an environment conducive to evolution, reflection, and innovation.

5.4. Strategies to Foster Consistent Growth

To master the art of perseverance and thereby facilitate consistent growth, consider the following strategies:

1. Develop a growth mindset: Strongly believe in your ability to grow beyond your existing capabilities and rise above challenges. This mindset fosters a sense of resilience and adaptability, fueling your persistence.

2. Set SMART goals: Specific, Measurable, Achievable, Relevant, and Time-bound goals provide clear direction and a sense of purpose, propelling your growth journey.

3. Embrace failure: Failure isn't the end but a learning opportunity. By embracing failure, you mold resilience and strengthen your resolve to grow.

4. Mindful tracking: Regularly monitor your progress, meeting successes with gratitude and setbacks with lessons to learn. Keeps your growth journey grounded and realistic.

Through these strategies, your consistent growth can become an inspiring testament to the power of perseverance.

5.5. Your Growth, Your Legacy

Indeed, the journey of steady growth—watered by the streams of perseverance—is a full circle connecting your current self to your potential and ultimately to your legacy. Every step climbed, every valley crossed, represents a resonating echo of your perseverance, shaping the narrative of your legacy.

In essence, mastering the art of perseverance and nurturing consistent growth isn't merely about achieving milestones. It is about evolving into the best version of yourself. It's about opening up to countless opportunities, inspiring others through your journey, leaving a mark on the world, and most importantly, living the legacy you were always meant to leave behind. Let your life be a beacon, a legendary tale of growth and perseverance replete with vibrant lessons for aspiring changemakers. Such indeed is the life imbued with purpose, impact, and a lasting legacy.

Chapter 6. Empowering Relationships: Building Your Circle of Influence

In order to navigate the labyrinthine journey of life, we need others to aid us, encouragement to boost us, and partnerships to enhance us. Building an empowering circle of influence is not merely about surrounding oneself with a plethora of personalities, but rather about deliberately choosing those individuals who augment our lives, who fuel our endeavors, and who echo the values we hold dear. Embarking on this journey, we begin to understand how our circle of influence augments our potential, reinforces our focus and shapes our legacy.

6.1. The Significance of Your Circle

In physics, the 'influence' in the circle of influence could be likened to the gravitational pull, a sort of intangible tether that, while unseen, undeniably shapes the paths we take. This is akin to the influence people around us hold. The ideas we absorb, the habits we adopt, and the decisions we make are often profoundly influenced by the people we interact with regularly.

In the larger narrative of building a life of purpose and impact, your circle of influence is akin to the scaffolding surrounding a building under construction. They provide structure, reinforce strength, offer support, and give form to your growing stature. Consequently, an empowering circle can accelerate your personal development, mitigate the vicissitudes of your journey, initiate fortuitous opportunities, and bolster the impact you make.

6.2. Selecting Your Circle: A Deliberate Pursuit

Selecting your circle of influence is a task of utmost significance that calls for deliberate action. You have a say in choosing who can share your personal space, who you allow to influence your thoughts, emotions, and actions. Start by identifying the traits that you value highly in others and that facilitate your growth. Perhaps you prioritize honesty, drivenness, altruism, or creativity—values that mirror your personal and legacy-oriented goals.

From acquaintances to close relations, assess from a larger perspective—whom do you admire? Whose company fuels your spirit, and whose presence challenges you positively? Whom do you witness demonstrating the values you cherish? These considerations form the essence of selecting your circle—an ongoing, yet fulfilling pursuit.

6.3. Nurturing Your Relationships

The longevity and strength of relationships within your circle of influence hinge upon one keyword: nurturing. Like nurturing a tender sapling to maturity, fostering relationships require patience, careful attention, and commitment.

Practice active listening – it positions you as a sincere confidante. Be genuinely interested in their life experiences, challenges, dreams, and perspectives. Keep judgements at bay, for they hamper real understanding of these individuals– your allies on the journey towards legacy building. Appreciate their uniqueness and respect the diversity they bring to your circle. Mutual honesty and constructive criticism help you grow, while fostering deep trust within your circle.

6.4. Building A Circle that Inspires

An inspirational circle of influence can catalyze a positive ripple effect into your journey of living the legacy. Seek individuals who are also in pursuit of their personal growth, whose actions reflect their dedication towards worthwhile ideals. Surround yourself with contagious enthusiasm, persistent resilience, unwavering commitment, and quiet compassion. People who personify these virtues and practice these actions inspire others with their own legacy, which in turn, can galvanize your path to purposeful living.

6.5. The Circle and Your Legacy

Remember, the ultimate goal isn't to merely have a circle. The goal is to have a circle that enhances your life, adds to your journeys, and helps in building and living your legacy. It isn't about having people who will sing your praises undeterred. Rather, it's about having people who appreciate your merits and yet are valorous enough to point out when you deviate from your path.

Your circle of influence becomes an integral part of your journey– a part of the legacy you wish to leave. When you engage in meaningful conversations, expose yourself to new perspectives, and embrace diversity, you render a depth and breadth to your personal legacy. Your circle might end up being the co-sculptors of the monument that your legacy eventually becomes.

In summation, building an empowering circle of influence is an expedition of awareness, deliberation, nurturing, inspiration, and mutual growth. It translates into creating a resonant support system which influences not just your present moment, but your path towards the pursuit of living and leaving a meaningful legacy behind.

Chapter 7. Your Actions Speak: Nurturing Impactful Habits

It is intrinsic to human nature to be governed by habits. Habits are the invisible architecture of everyday life that shape who we are and who we can become, guiding us on our path towards purpose and impact. These are the subconscious choices we make each day that cement our paths toward success or, on the flip side, steer us into stagnation. Thoughtfully cultivating impactful habits fosters a life of remarkable achievements, profound growth, and lasting legacy.

7.1. Embracing the Power of Habits

Reminiscent of the phrase "Actions speak louder than words", our habits are the embodiment of our internal belief systems, values, and personal mission. They are the microscopic gears driving the mechanisms of our lives. For instance, if you're in the habit of waking up early, it illustrates your reverence for the sanctity of time; if you routinely partake in charitable works, it highlights your heart for service. Whether we acknowledge it or not, our habits are declarations of our character, underwriting the pages of our legacy.

To foster impactful habits, you must acknowledge their potential for transformative power. Begin by developing an appreciation for the influence that even the simplest routines can have. Just as a single piece of Lego can contribute to crafting an intricate structure, each minor habit amounts to significant change over time.

7.2. The Habit Loop: Understand, Dissect, Recreate

The 'Habit Loop' forms the structural anatomy of any habit, comprised essentially of three main components—a Cue, a Routine and a Reward. The cue is a trigger that initiates the routine, which is the action we perform. Lastly, the reward is what we obtain from performing the routine. By comprehending the nuances of this structure, we can dissect our current habits and deliberately recreate more beneficial ones.

Start by observing your current habits; jot down the cues, routines, and rewards. Regularly analyze these entries to identify patterns or room for improvement. For example, if you notice a habit of snacking on unhealthy foods after office hours (Routine), triggered by craving something sweet (Cue), resulting in instant gratification (Reward), you could substitute the unhealthy snack with a healthier option, thereby preserving the cue and reward but altering the routine to a healthier choice.

7.3. Building a Routine of Impactful Habits

After dissecting your habits, the next crucial step is to construct a routine teeming with impactful habits. This is a combination of deducting detrimental habits while adopting beneficial ones. However, it's essential to recognize that this overhaul is not a switch to flip overnight but a steady, careful process that happens over time.

Begin by defining clear objectives—what habits you want to adopt and why. The 'why' serves as the core motivation that propels you forward, especially during periods of resistance. The more personalized the 'why' is, the stronger its driving force.

Consider using tools like habit stacking or the two-minute rule, both techniques proposed in James Clear's 'Atomic Habits'. Habit stacking involves linking a new habit to an already existing one. For instance, if you wish to incorporate reading into your routine, stack it onto an existing habit like having your morning coffee. On the other hand, the two-minute rule encourages taking small steps. If you aim to write a book, start with writing for just two minutes every day and gradually increase the time.

These techniques alleviate the process of habit formation, making your journey towards impactful habits an achievable endeavor.

7.4. Resilience: Your Companion in the Journey

The journey of cultivating impactful habits is occasionally speckled with hardship. There might be moments when you falter, or times when the desired result seems elusive. It's during these moments that resilience is your best companion. Resilience is the internal strength that allows you to navigate through setbacks, to dust off your past mistakes, and to persist towards your goals with renewed determination.

Remember, every round of failure or setback is not a step backwards, but a detour leading you to the door of self-understanding and growth. Each stumble is an opportunity to reassess, realign and press forward with an evolved understanding and a resilient spirit.

7.5. Leaving a Legacy through Your Habits

The sum of our daily habits, both microscopic and monumental, braided together with the threads of consistency and resilience, weaves the tapestry of our legacy. Your commitment to nurturing impactful habits resonates beyond the quotidian, impacting others either directly through your interactions or indirectly through the example you set.

Take charge of your actions, cultivate habits consciously, and remember – every choice you make, every habit you instill, is an act of authoring the story that will be your legacy. Myriads of seemingly ordinary actions, bridled together, construct an extraordinary life of purpose and impact. You leave a legacy not just by what you accomplish, but by how you live, and habits form the bedrock of this living.

Indeed, nurturing impactful habits is far from a trivial pursuit; it is a voyage into the heart of a life lived consciously, laced with purpose and echoed in legacy. It is an anthem of positive transformation, a beacon of personal growth, and truly, the heart-line of your legacy.

Chapter 8. Wellness for Life: The Vitality of Physical and Mental Health

In the radiant course of life, we are called to maintain a dual-edged vitality: physical and mental. These two combined hold the characteristic of being the beating heart fueling the voyage towards living your legacy. Living an impactful life is no small feat, and it needs a robust, healthy vessel to carry it. Just as a ship requires the brawny strength of its sails as well as the contained mettle of its crew to chart treacherous waters successfully, you require both physical and mental wellness to fuel your journey towards living your legacy.

8.1. The Parity of Physical and Mental Health

Fostering physical and mental health isn't a process filled with smooth sailings. Ups and downs punctuate its course, each challenge a testament to resilience and tenacity. At its core, physical health brims with the verve and vigor that directly affect the way you feel, look, and show up in the world, while mental health, on the other hand, has a ripple effect on your thoughts, emotions, and overall perspective.

Just as a robust and resonant building relies on the strength and stability of its foundation and framework, healthiness ensues from the harmonious balance between physical and mental wellness, each underpinning the other, each influencing the other. You need to be physically fit to generate the energy required for mental workout. In turn, mental wellness champions a healthier lifestyle through fostering resilience, managing stress more effectively, and promoting healthier decision-making. It's crucial to cast an equally discerning eye on both sides of the spectrum and formulate strategies that simultaneously emphasize their mutual development.

8.2. A Robust Regiment for Physical Wellness

Physical wellness can be likened to the mighty oak that withstands storms, its roots deep in the ground and its branches soaring the skies. This durable resistance stems from an optimal mix of regular physical activity, balanced nutrition, appropriate rest, and preventative healthcare.

Regular physical activity, one of the key components of physical wellness, may include moderate aerobics, strength, and resistance exercises. These exercises strengthen muscles, improve cardiovascular health, maintain flexibility, and manage body weight.

Balanced nutrition supplies the body with necessary nutrients, thus providing much needed energy, supporting bodily functions, strengthening the immune system, and promoting the body's recovery capabilities.

Sleep, too, is fundamental to physical health. It's when our bodies rejuvenate, repair tissues, synthesize hormones, and consolidate memory. Sleep deficiencies can lead to a host of health problems ranging from depression, poor concentration, weakened immunity to chronic diseases like diabetes and heart disease.

Preventative healthcare involves regular check-ups, vaccinations, and screenings to identify health issues early.

8.3. The Landscape of Mental Wellness

Just as the sun's fragile rays at dawn gain enough strength to light the world, the path to mental wellness isn't without formidable hurdles. These obstacles fail to dim the radiance of a completely achievable goal: a state of mental well-being where each individual realizes their potential, copes with normal life stresses, works productively, and contributes to their community.

Key enablers fostering mental wellness include stress management, emotional self-care, and maintaining a positive outlook towards life.

Stress management is indeed a critical aspect of mental wellness, as long-term unmanaged stress can culminate in emotional, physical, and mental health problems. Adopting stress-relief techniques such as mindfulness, meditation, yoga, deep breathing, and physical exercises can be significantly effective.

Emotional self-care, in turn, involves recognizing and acknowledging your feelings, accepting your imperfections, setting boundaries, and taking time for activities that you enjoy.

And lastly, resilience and a positive outlook helps one navigate through the vicissitudes of life, view challenges as opportunities rather than threats, and boost emotional well-being.

8.4. Merging The Two: A Synchronized Symphony

Just as a perfectly synchronized symphony is only possible when each instrument plays its part in harmony, creating a sonorous symphony of life involves playing the mental and physical health instruments harmoniously—which is not merely about preventing illness but more about proactive strategies that promote wellness at both levels.

Physical exercises, known to release 'feel-good' endorphins, play a key role in alleviating stress, depression, and anxiety, while aspects of mental wellness such as resilience, stress management, and a positive attitude encourage healthier lifestyle choices leading to improved physical wellness.

Ultimately, it's important to realize that mental and physical health are interwoven strands in the fabric of our overall health. Investing time and diligence in maintaining this comprehensive wellness can enable you to steer the ship of your life more effectively, clear mental fog, unlock higher energy levels, and embody the prime version of yourself.

8.5. Your Legacy and Your Wellness

Living your legacy demands a well-maintained engine that keeps running, even when challenged with the long stretches of the journey. This engine is a perfect blend of physical and mental wellness. As you design a life packed with purpose and impact, remember that your legacy isn't solely about what you achieve—it's about who you become in the process.

Choosing to invest in your health is choosing to invest in your legacy. Because a healthier you doesn't just live longer— it lives better. By prioritizing wellness, you open up possibilities for longevity, enhanced performance, increased productivity, joy, and a vibrant life—the vital ingredients needed for anyone aspiring to leave a profound impact on the world.

Chapter 9. The Power of Giving: Social Responsibility and Charity

In our ceaseless quest for personal growth and success, it is crucial not to lose sight of the extraordinary power of altruism, philanthropy, and community service. This chapter delves into the essential roles that social responsibility and charity play—not only in shaping our character but also in leaving a distinctive, long-lasting legacy.

9.1. Embracing the Spirit of Giving

The pathway towards a life marked by purpose and impact inherently intersects with the principles of social responsibility and charity. This powerful relationship is underpinned by the exponential potential found in the act of giving. Charity is not constrained to financial donations; it extends to all forms of giving—time, effort, knowledge, and resources. It's about offering something valuable to those who need it the most, thus planting the seeds of compassion, empathy, and positive change in society.

Understanding the importance of giving and aligning our actions with this practice imparts a sense of expansive fulfillment that's unattainable through personal achievements alone. There's a certain kind of enrichment that comes from enhancing the lives of others, igniting sparks of hope, and contributing to a broader narrative of societal advancement and unity. It is this experience of meaningful contribution that gives rise to a deeper sense of fulfillment, fostering personal growth while strengthening bonds within our community.

9.2. Everything You Do Matters: Social Responsibility as a Way of Life

Social responsibility encapsulates our commitment towards the greater good. It is an embodiment of understanding that our decisions and actions have consequences that echo beyond our individual spheres. Every choice we make, every action we take, can have profound consequences, sowing seeds that curate the quality of life and society for years or even decades to come.

Recognizing that our actions are potent instruments for change is a vital step towards living responsibly. From daily interactions with people around us to decisions we make in our professional realm, everything counts. Often, it is the small gestures of kindness, respect, or fairness that exact the most meaningful influence on others and shape the fabric of our communities and societies.

However, transforming this understanding into reality requires conscious and consistent effort. Social responsibility is not a one-time act, but a way of living, a mindset that we need to cultivate and nurture. Thus, it's essential to incorporate socially responsible practices into our daily routines, workplaces, and relationships.

9.3. Charity Begins at Home: Cultivating an Environment of Generosity

Charity, like any other virtue, is not innate but rather cultivated and nurtured through persistent practice and intentional cultivation. To transition from merely understanding the significance of charity to actively practicing it, we must first cultivate personal moments of generosity, even within the confines of our own homes or immediate surroundings.

Seize opportunities to practice acts of kindness and generosity in your daily life. It's vital to remind ourselves that charity isn't just about monumental acts of giving but is also steeped in little deeds of goodness that we can accommodate in our routine without much ado.

Offer help, share knowledge, be there for someone in need—in essence, nurture an environment of generosity around you. This fostering of a charitable spirit has a domino effect. As we perpetually and genuinely engage in acts of giving, we elucidate a personal example, inspiring others to adopt similar practices, thereby amplifying the impact manifold.

9.4. Building Bridges: Aligning Social Responsibility and Charity with Professional Life

Aligning charitable endeavors and principles of social responsibility with our professional life imparts a multidimensional effect. In addition to personal fulfillment, it fosters a culture of empathy, compassion, and social awareness within organizations, augments brand reputation, and invariably influences consumer behavior in favor of such socially conscious organizations.

Implementing Corporate Social Responsibility (CSR) initiatives, encouraging employees to undertake volunteer work, and integrating sustainable practices are all mechanisms to achieve this alignment. Not only will they enhance the legacy you're creating, but they also help build a more resilient society.

9.5. The Ripple Effect: Giving Paves the Way for a Better World

Indeed, social responsibility and charity have a ripple effect, resonating across boundaries and eventually manifesting as positive transformation in the world at large. By fueling a chain reaction of goodness, these actions contribute to the creation of a more harmonious, equitable, and sustainable world. They are our moral compass, guiding us towards making decisions that honor our purpose and affirm our commitment to creating meaningful change.

The power of giving, hence, is more than personal. It transcends our immediate existence and trickles down to our interactions, our environment, our societies, and most importantly, our legacy. It offers us the extraordinary opportunity to play an active role in the world's betterment, and this is the legacy that endures—an echo of our existence that continues to reverberate long after we're gone.

As we conclude this chapter on social responsibility and charity, we are left pondering the remarkable potential lying within giving. By embracing the principles of charity and social responsibility and incorporating them into our lives, we embark on a journey toward cementing a legacy that truly matters—one that amplifies the best of humanity and continues to influence long after we are no more. The challenge, therefore, lies in not just understanding this but translating it into consistent habits, actions, and choices. May this realization guide us on our fulfilling journey towards 'Living The Legacy'.

Chapter 10. Living The Legacy: Being an Example Everyday

Every day presents an immense opportunity for you to paint your legacy on the canvas of time, to be the torchbearer of values, aspirations, and goals that may reverberate far beyond your individual life. Being an example every day is a profound step in living your legacy, a profound task that involves leading by example, authenticity, and continual growth. It's not merely a declarative statement of intent but an active pursuit in transforming thought into tangible action and ultimately, lasting legacy.

10.1. Embodying Your Core Values

Becoming a living embodiment of your core values is a cornerstone to being an example every day. Turning points and moments of introspection often define these values. Yet, consistency in action and thought during everyday situations truly emulates them. Perhaps your core values entail kindness, learning, or resilience; it isn't the grand gestures but consistent conduct in both limelight and solitude that speak volumes.

Imagine you value truth and honesty. When tempted to bend a seemingly inconsequential truth for comfort or gain, standing firm in honoring your value renders you an everyday example of honesty. Being an exemplification of your values isn't an easy endeavor—it may require disclaimers, it may puzzle onlookers, and at times, it may even isolate you. Yet, each testing of your resolve strengthens your legacy, forged in the crucible of daily choice.

10.2. Being Authentic

Authenticity is the soul of a legacy. The masks worn for society and oneself often obscure the authentic self. Dropping these masks demands courage. It is a journey of acknowledging faults, fostering strengths, and continually evolving to embody the 'authentic' version of oneself. Society may demand conformity, yet every day you live authentically, you refute these unreal expectations, broadening the definition of what it is to inhabit your true self. This authenticity resonates the unique cadence of your legacy, echoing through the hearts and minds you touch in your journey.

10.3. Fostering Constant Growth

Growth should not be a mere byproduct of time, but a cultivation of conscious effort. Constant growth propels us towards becoming the paragon of our visions. Embrace every endeavor, each failure, and little success as pivotal elements contributing to your evolution - where challenges are not dead-ends but stepping stones, and comfort zones merely represent the starting line. Every day, strive for self-improvement, refining wisdom, fostering empathy, and acquiring novel skills or perspectives. While this may appear mammoth from afar, it starts with basic daily practices like reflective thought, openness to feedback, and a genuine appetite for learning.

10.4. Cultivating Impactful Actions

A cornerstone of living your legacy every day lies in plying actions that lay a stone onto the edifice of your legacy. These actions needn't be lead stories of a news hour; instead, they are everyday actions intertwined with kindness, resilience, honesty, or other such values that you hold dear. You can offer help before it's requested, you can choose to recycle predicting future accumulation, or you can dedicate time towards mentoring someone. A cyclone might be remembered for the destruction it leaves behind, but it's the everyday wind that shapes the dunes over time.

10.5. Mindfulness & Stewardship

Legacy doesn't merely belong to a certain few but is within the grasps of each one of us. Being mindful of our actions, their ripples, and taking ownership is crucial. This involves knowing that every choice, word, or action, no matter how trivial, shaped the world around us, impacting the lives of others. Understand that stewardship isn't about control but nurturing, looking after our shared world, and fostering a better tomorrow. Practice stewardship not just in moments of glory or crisis, but in banal routines and mundane tasks.

In conclusion, 'Living The Legacy: Being an Example Everyday' encapsulates the transformative journey that pivots on daily actions sustained by core values, authenticity, growth, and stewardship. It's an invitation to cultivate your legacy every day, throughout the ordinary and extraordinary, for a legacy isn't built on intent alone but action's fruition. As you look back, you won't find your legacy confined to the crowning moments but woven into the fabric of your everyday life; and in there, you'll find your most profound self, quietly living a legacy that reverberates through time.

Chapter 11. Preserving Your Legacy: Impact Today, Influence Tomorrow

In the grand tapestry of time and space, it's the exquisite embroidery of our actions, stitched with the thread of intent and purpose, that forms the imperishable pattern of our legacy. All the chapters preceding this have led you down the path of self-discovery and self-empowerment—each one a stepping-stone towards becoming your highest self. While the journey is intrinsic and fundamentally enriching, its ultimate purpose is its outward manifestation—Preserving Your Legacy. This chapter is dedicated to total immersion in the process of impacting today and influencing tomorrow. It is here that all your vision, growth, and strategies coalesce into a poignant reality—the creation and preservation of your legacy!

11.1. The Definition and Importance of Legacy

Before we can delve deep into the preservation of our legacy, let's take a moment to explore what legacy truly means. In broad strokes, your legacy is the ripple effect of your existence. It is the footprint you leave behind—not in sand, but in the hearts and minds of people, and most enduringly, in the shape and trajectory of society. It is the sum total of your actions, ambitions, teachings, and their resultant outcomes. More personal than reputation, and transcending mere material wealth, your legacy is your life's message to the world. Possessing a transformative, eternal character, it allows you to live beyond your physical death. It's the essence of true immortality.

This never-ending ripple is not an accident or byproduct of life, but a consciously created reality. Its gravitas stresses the crucial importance of its preservation for the dual purpose of making an immediate impact and securing a long-lasting influence. Despite residing in the future realm, this imminent influence is brought to life in the present, breathed into every act today. Hence, to successfully preserve a legacy, we need an acute awareness that every action (or inaction), every choice, every word casts a stone, setting the ripples into motion.

11.2. Legacy Preservation: Step-by-Step Strategy

The process of preserving your legacy can be viewed as a strategic mission. We can break down this mission into clear, actionable steps.

1. **Document your legacy:** Reflect on your philosophy, goals, key moments, and lessons learned. Document these in a journal or video logs. They serve as clarifying tools for self-understanding and provide valuable insights for those who will carry your torch forward.

2. **Live your legacy daily:** The most powerful propaganda for your legacy is your lifestyle. Apply your values to everything you do. Be consistent with your beliefs and demonstrate them daily through your actions, decisions, and interactions.

3. **Amplify Impact Through Others:** Your capacity to impact others defines your legacy's strength. Teach, mentor, inspire, and empower those around you. Share your knowledge, experiences, and wisdom. Your legacy thrives when others incorporate your teachings into their lives.

4. **Remember, Everything Counts:** Each word, each action, however minute, contributes to your legacy. Unexpected moments often leave the deepest impressions. Strive for integrity and authenticity not just in big things but in all things.

5. **Leave a Material Manifestation:** Consider leaving a legacy fund, or creating an organization that encapsulates your cause or vision. This becomes a tangible testimony to your beliefs and serves as a vehicle to facilitate your influence beyond your physical existence.

11.3. A Living Legacy: Impact Today

A good portion of legacy preservation lies in our ability to create substantial impact today. Engaging in meaningful activities that reflect our core values and contribute positively to our surroundings is key. We are not merely living for posterity; we are living for today—making each day a testament to what we stand for. In fact, manifesting your legacy today serves a dual purpose. Firstly, it validates your purpose, embodies your vision, and creates immediate effects that validate your mission and goals in the 'now'. Secondly, nothing builds legacy better than a pattern of consistent evidence—you become reliable, dependable, and trustworthy.

11.4. An Echoing Influence: Impact Tomorrow

While our daily impacts largely define our legacy, the other undefinable aspect is the potential to influence tomorrow. This subtle, yet powerful impact echoes through time, often untouched by the physical boundaries of life. The question of longevity prompts us to introspect—What will remain when we are no longer present in physical form? Will our legacy continue to inspire, ignite and influence?

Creating a lasting legacy requires strategic planning. Establish structures for your goals and ideals that will withstand time. Use education, mentorship, and successions plans to ensure continuity of your ideas and wisdom. Crafting this influence is not an exact science; the anatomy of each legacy is unique, shaped by life and fed by a ceaseless supply of passion and purpose.

In conclusion, as this chapter eloquently declares, the preservation of your legacy pivots on the fulcrum of your everyday life. Be present to the weightage of your actions; they are the architects of tomorrow. Make every day a tribute to your ultimate purpose, a dance with destiny that passionately whispers to the world: "This is my legacy!" Today's influence, tomorrow's impact— donned on your life like a celebratory mantle, they champion your grand narrative, the essence of your being, in the labyrinth of legacy. This is the climactic chapter in your grand opus. Seize it, live it, and most importantly, preserve it. Be that illustrious beacon of inspiration—the living epitome of a truly purposeful life.

www.ingramcontent.com/pod-product-compliance
Lightning Source LLC
Chambersburg PA
CBHW072218290526
45794CB00007B/2793